Accent on Achievement

John O'Reilly and **Mark Williams**

A comprehensive band method that develops creativity and musicianship

Dear Band Student:

Congratulations on deciding to become a member of the **band**! There is a special kind of enjoyment that comes from performing with a musical group that can be found nowhere else. As a skilled band musician, you will be able to play a wide variety of musical styles from **symphony** to **jazz**, from **contemporary pop** to **marching band**. With regular daily practice, there's no limit to the exciting musical experiences waiting for you! We wish you the best of success in achieving your musical goals.

John O'Reilly

Mark Williams

Art Direction: Ruth Lebenson
Book Design: Tom Gerou
Music Engraving: Greg Plumblee
Illustrations: Martin Ledyard
Photography (pages 3 & 4): Jordan Miller

Instrument photos (cover, pages 1 & 2) are courtesy of Yamaha Corporation of America.
Thanks to the students and staff of Lindero Canyon Middle School and Band Director Matt McKagan for their participation in the photographs on pages 3 and 4.

D1378847

GETTING READY TO PLAY

1. Cane reeds should be soaked in 1 inch of water for a minimum of 3 minutes before playing. A plastic 35mm film container is excellent for soaking your reeds. Bassoon reeds should only be soaked up to the first wire. (Synthetic reeds do not need to be soaked.)

2. Apply a small quantity of cork grease to each cork (or winding), as necessary.

3. Holding the boot joint in your right hand, insert the long joint using a back and forth twisting motion so that the long keys are facing the same direction as the large round key on the boot joint.

4. Holding the assembled boot and long joints in your left hand, carefully add the tenor joint. Connect the tenor and long joints together with the locking mechanism, if available.

5.. Press down the key on the bell and add the bell to the long joint, lining up the bridge keys. Attach the seat strap (or neck strap) to the instrument.

6. Hold the bocal near the cork and gently twist into place, so that the vent hole is lined up with the whisper key pad. Blow through the reed to remove excess water, and carefully put the reed onto the bocal.

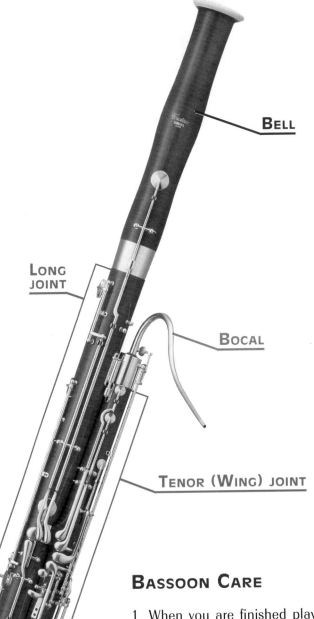

BELL

LONG JOINT

BOCAL

TENOR (WING) JOINT

BOOT JOINT

HAND REST

BASSOON CARE

1. When you are finished playing, take off the reed and blow out the excess moisture. Place it in a well-ventilated reed holder to dry. Remove the bocal and blow through the large end to remove the moisture.

2. Use a bassoon swab to dry the inside of the tenor joint. Pour excess moisture from the small end of the boot joint and swab. The other sections usually do not require swabbing.

3. To keep your keys shiny, wipe them off with a soft cloth.

4. Store only those items in your case that the case is designed to hold. Forcing music or other objects into your bassoon case can cause problems with the instrument.

CHECK YOUR PLAYING POSITION

1. Sit on the front half of your chair.
2. Keep your feet flat on the floor.
3. Sit up straight and tall.
4. Adjust the seat strap (or neck strap) so that the instrument feels balanced on a diagonal in front of you and the reed falls comfortably into your mouth when you tip your head slightly forward.
5. Adjust the height of the hand rest so that your right hand fingers can easily cover the tone holes. Use of the hand rest is optional when using a seat strap.
6. Fingers remain curved, even when not pressing down keys or covering holes.

FORMING THE EMBOUCHURE

Embouchure (ahm'-buh-sure) is a French word used to describe the way you shape your mouth while playing. Here is how to form a good embouchure:

1. Relax your lower jaw and pull it back, so that the upper lip is ahead of the lower lip.
2. Roll your upper and lower lips over your teeth to provide a cushion for the reed. Place the reed in your mouth so that your upper lip almost touches the first wire.
3. Support the reed with your lips, using even, gentle pressure from all sides, like a rubber band. Keep your lower jaw open and back so that there is no pressure from your lower teeth.

PRODUCING YOUR FIRST TONE

1. Practice taking a full breath, filling the bottom of your lungs so that your stomach expands. Then fill the top of your lungs without raising your shoulders. With gentle pressure, exhale completely. Always using a full breath while playing helps to produce long, full tones.
2. Our first tone will be produced using just the reed. Hold the reed in the correct position for playing, form an embouchure and take a full breath through the corners of your mouth. Lift your tongue so that it touches the tip of the reed. Now start to exhale and then release the reed with your tongue as if saying "Too". Make the tone last as long as possible. Next, produce several notes on one breath by touching the reed with your tongue as if saying "Too-Too-Too-Too—" while exhaling. Produce as many notes as possible on one breath until you run out of air.

PRACTICE TIPS

1. Try to find a place with a good, firm chair where you will not be interrupted. Use a music stand to hold your music in the correct position for playing.
2. Occasionally use different reeds so that you will always have more than one reed ready for performance.
3. Start by playing long tones. This builds your embouchure and improves your tone.
4. Always include some already learned "review" pieces, so that you continue to improve and perfect your performance.
5. Spend a concentrated period of time on the most difficult parts of your music. Avoid the temptation to play only the easy parts.
6. To make your practice even more enjoyable, try playing along with the ***ACCENT ON ACHIEVEMENT*** accompaniment CDs or cassettes.

THE STAFF

5 lines and 4 spaces used for writing music.

BASS CLEF

Also called F clef. The fourth line of the staff is the note F.

TIME SIGNATURE

Tells us how many beats are in a measure and what kind of note gets one beat.

BAR LINE

Divides the staff into measures.

MEASURE

The distance between two bar lines.

DOUBLE BAR

The end of a section of music.

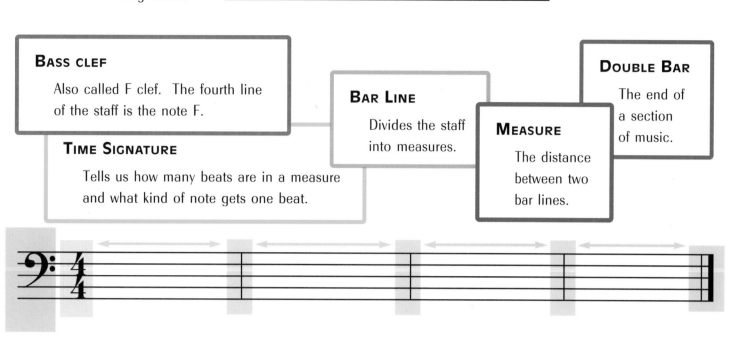

THE MUSICAL ALPHABET

The musical alphabet uses only the letters A through G. These are used to name the notes on the staff in **LINE-SPACE-LINE-SPACE** order (A, B, C, D, E, F, G, A, B, etc.). There are rules that help us remember the names of the lines and spaces of the staff.

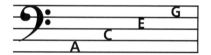

The spaces can be remembered by using the first letter of each word in the sentence **All Cows Eat Grass.**

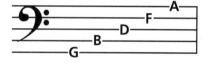

The lines can be remembered by using the first letter of each word in the sentence **Good Boys Do Fine Always.**

LEDGER LINES

Used to extend the staff.

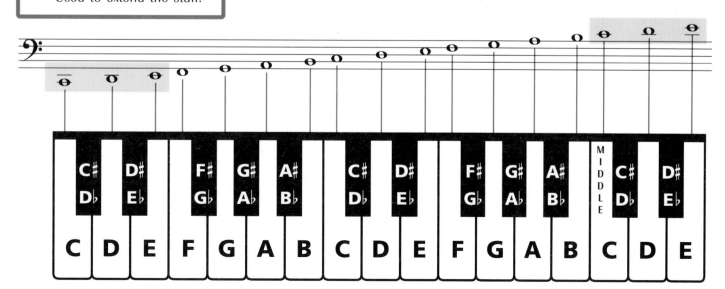

SOLO
One person playing

TIME SIGNATURE
4 = 4 beats in each measure
4 = quarter note receives 1 beat

WHOLE NOTE
1 & 2 & 3 & 4 &
Receives 4 beats in **4/4** time.

WHOLE REST
1 & 2 & 3 & 4 &
Indicates a whole measure of silence.

FLAT
Lowers the pitch of a note one half step.

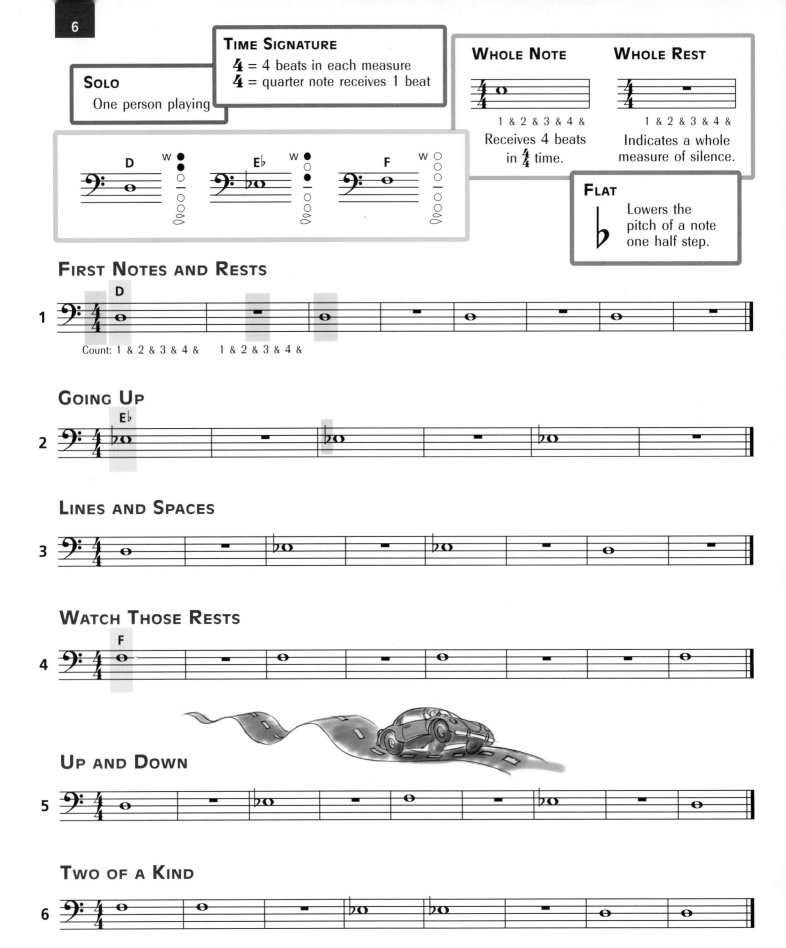

FIRST NOTES AND RESTS

1. Count: 1 & 2 & 3 & 4 &   1 & 2 & 3 & 4 &

GOING UP

2.

LINES AND SPACES

3.

WATCH THOSE RESTS

4.

UP AND DOWN

5.

TWO OF A KIND

6.

ACCENT ON LISTENING

Listen carefully to the soloist, then match the pitch.

7.

SOLO   BAND   SOLO   BAND   SOLO   BAND   SOLO   BAND

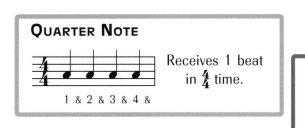

QUARTER NOTE

Receives 1 beat in 4/4 time.

DUET

A composition with parts for two players.

BREATH MARK ,

A suggested place to take a breath.

GOOD NEIGHBORS

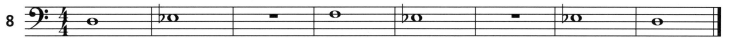

MIX 'EM UP

FOUR IN A ROW

Also Eb

Count: 1 & 2 & 3 & 4 &

PASSING NOTES (Duet)

TAKE FIVE

THREE-NOTE SAMBA

ACCENT ON THEORY Fill in the note names, then fill in the fingerings.

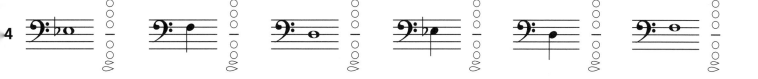

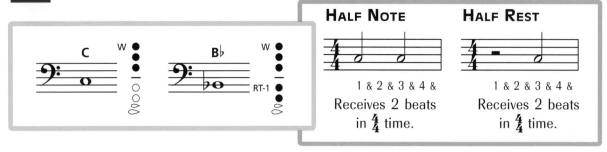

MOVIN' ON DOWN

HALF FULL OR HALF EMPTY (Duet)

HOT CROSS BUNS

English Folk Song

AU CLAIRE DE LA LUNE

French Folk Song

JINGLE BELLS

Traditional Carol

ACCENT ON LISTENING

1. Play "Mary Had a Little Lamb" by ear.
2. Write in the missing notes to complete the song.

QUARTER REST

Receives 1 beat in 2/4 and 4/4 time.

1 & 2 &

REPEAT SIGN :||
Play the music again from the beginning.

TIME SIGNATURE
2 = 2 beats in each measure
4 = quarter note receives 1 beat

ROUND
Playing the same music beginning at different times.

HANDCLAPPER'S MARCH

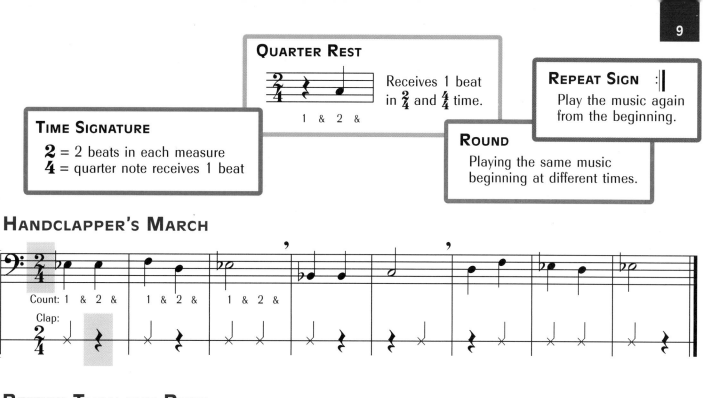

Count: 1 & 2 &   1 & 2 &   1 & 2 &

Clap:

BETTER THAN THE REST
Clap first, then play.

GOOD KING WENCESLAS
Traditional Carol

DONKEY ROUND
American Folk Song

DREYDL, DREYDL
Traditional Hanukkah Song

ACCENT ON BASSOON

For more individual technique practice, see page 42, #1.

TIE

Joins two notes of the same pitch to make one long note.

1 & 2 & 1 & 2 &

KEY SIGNATURE

Indicates notes which are to be flatted or sharped. All B's and E's should be played as B♭ and E♭ throughout.

TEMPO MARKINGS

Moderato **Allegro**

Medium tempo   Fast tempo

REACHING DOWN

27

THE SCORE IS TIED (Duet)

a

28

b

1 & 2 &   1 & 2 &

MARY ANN

Jamaican Folk Song

Moderato

29

SHOO, FLY

American Folk Song

Allegro

30

ACCENT ON THEORY: *On the Bridge at Avignon*

Name the notes, then play.

French Folk Song

31

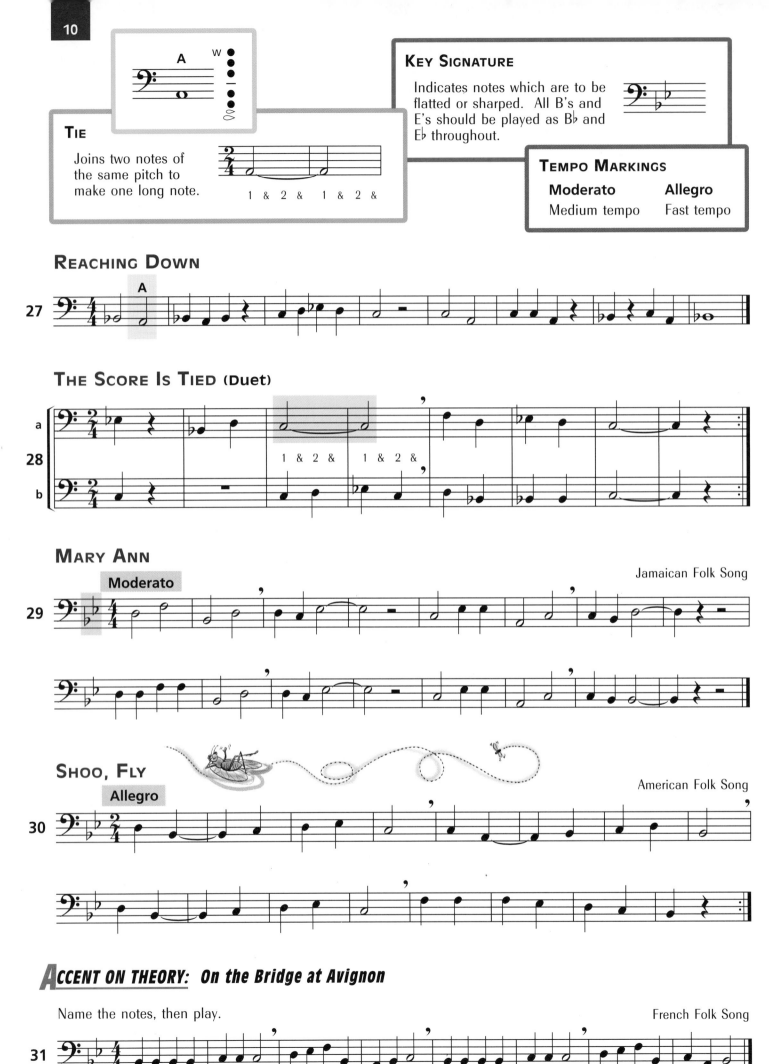

ACCENT ON PERFORMANCE

HOLIDAY SAMPLER

Arr. by John O'Reilly
and Mark Williams

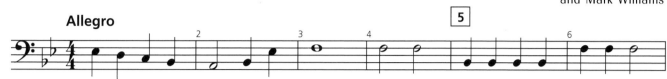

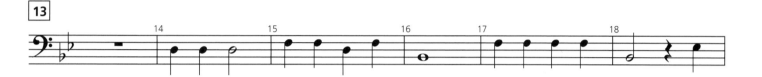

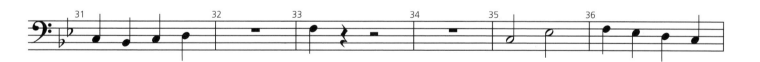

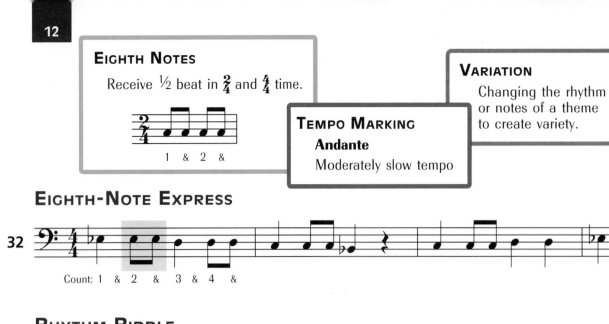

EIGHTH NOTES
Receive ½ beat in $\frac{2}{4}$ and $\frac{4}{4}$ time.

1 & 2 &

TEMPO MARKING
Andante
Moderately slow tempo

VARIATION
Changing the rhythm or notes of a theme to create variety.

EIGHTH-NOTE EXPRESS

32

Count: 1 & 2 & 3 & 4 &

RHYTHM RIDDLE

Clap first, then play.

33

BILE THEM CABBAGE DOWN

Allegro

American Fiddle Tune

34

SURPRISE SYMPHONY

Franz Joseph Haydn
(1732–1809)

THEME
Andante

35

VARIATION

ACCENT ON CREATIVITY: *Variation on Lightly Row*

Create your own variation by changing some of the quarter notes into pairs of eighth notes.

German Folk Song

36

INTERNAL REPEAT

Repeat only the music between the signs.

1st and 2nd Endings

2nd time: skip the first ending and play the second.

Climbing Higher

More Eighth Notes

London Bridge (Duet)

Moderato

English Folk Song

Stodola Pumpa

Czech Folk Song

Allegro

Skip to My Lou

American Folk Song

Moderato

First Chorale

Andante

ACCENT ON BASSOON

For more individual technique practice, see page 42, #2.

SLUR

"Too" ____

Connects notes of different pitch.

Tongue only the first note.

DOTTED HALF NOTE

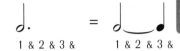

1 & 2 & 3 &   1 & 2 & 3 &

A dot following a note increases its length by ½ its original value.

In ¾ and 4/4 time, a dotted half note receives 3 beats.

DIVISI

Some players play the top notes while others play the bottom notes.

div.

TIME SIGNATURE

3 = 3 beats in each measure
4 = quarter note receives 1 beat

SLURS AND DOTS

44

THREE-FOUR DUET

a

45

b

SOUTHERN ROSES

Johann Strauss, Jr.
(1825–1899)

Moderato

46

MEXICAN JUMPING BEANS
(Variation on CHIAPANECAS)

Mexican Folk Song

Allegro

47

1.   2.   *div.*

ACCENT ON THEORY

Draw the correct bar lines, then play.

48

NATURAL

Cancels a flat or sharp until the next bar line.

KEY SIGNATURE

All B's should be played as B♭ throughout.

DYNAMIC MARKINGS

f   *p*

forte–loud   **piano**–soft

TWO WAYS TO PLAY IT

49

AURA LEE (Duet)

Andante   American Folk Song

a

50

b

FRÈRE JACQUES (Round)

Moderato   French Folk Song

51

MORNING from "PEER GYNT"

Edvard Grieg
(1843–1907)

Andante

52

ACCENT ON CREATIVITY: *Camptown Races*

Add your own dynamic markings, then perform.

Stephen Foster
(1826–1864)

a

3

Clap:

b

RITARDANDO
rit.
Gradually slow down the tempo.

FERMATA
Hold the note longer.

PICK-UP NOTES

(1 2 3) 4
Notes that precede the first full measure.

PATTERNS WITH PICK-UPS

CARNIVAL OF VENICE

Moderato

Italian Folk Song

JOLLY OLD ST. NICHOLAS

Allegro

Traditional Carol

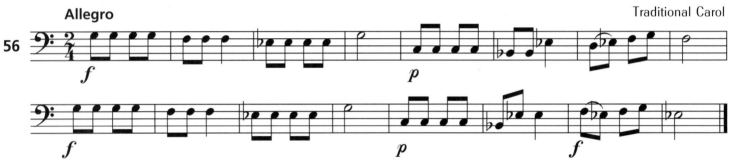

THE SNAKE CHARMER

Andante

Traditional

BILL GROGAN'S GOAT

Allegro

American Folk Song

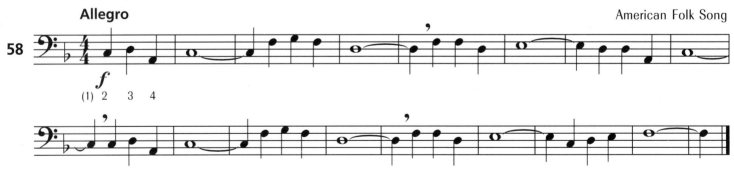

ACCENT ON BASSOON

For more individual technique practice, see page 42, #3 & 4.

ACCENT ON PERFORMANCE

EAGLE SUMMIT MARCH

John O'Reilly and
Mark Williams

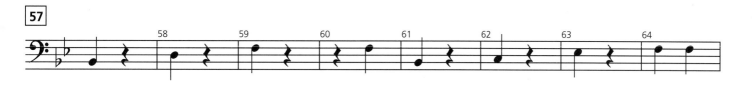

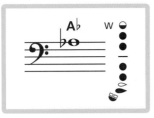

KEY SIGNATURE

All B's, E's and A's should be played as B♭, E♭ and A♭ throughout.

ANOTHER NEW NOTE

60

WHEN LOVE IS KIND

Irish Folk Song

Moderato

61

THEME FROM "SYMPHONY NO. 1"

Johannes Brahms (1833–1897)

Allegro

62

ALOHA 'OE

Queen Lili'uokalani (Hawaii) (1838–1917)

Andante

63

MINKA, MINKA

Ukrainian Folk Song

Moderato

a

64

Clap:

b

ACCENT ON THEORY

KEY RINGS: Circle all notes changed by the key signature.

65

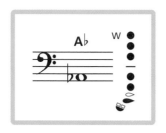

THE KEY MAKES THE DIFFERENCE

JASMINE FLOWER

Chinese Folk Song

ORCHESTRATION: Flute/Trumpet

Clarinet/Alto Sax

Low Brass/Low Woodwinds

Band

BLUES ADVENTURE (Duet)

ACCENT ON CREATIVITY: *This Old Man*

Choose your own orchestration for this melody.

American Folk Song

SINGLE EIGHTH NOTE AND EIGHTH REST

Each receives ½ beat in $\frac{2}{4}$, $\frac{3}{4}$ and $\frac{4}{4}$ time.

EASY EIGHTHS

70

POLLY WOLLY DOODLE

American Folk Song

71 Allegro

MARCH FROM "RONDO ALLA TURCA"

Wolfgang A. Mozart
(1756–1791)

72 Moderato

LA BAMBA

Mexican Folk Song

73 Allegro

div.

ACCENT ON BASSOON

74

For more individual technique practice, see page 42, #5.

TEMPO MARKING
Vivace
Very fast tempo

OPPOSITE DIRECTIONS

75

ACCIDENTAL ENCOUNTER

76

CHESTER

William Billings
(1746–1800)

Andante

77

BELLA BIMBA

Italian Folk Song

Moderato

78

CHOPSTICKS (Duet)

Traditional

Vivace

79

ACCENT ON THEORY   Fill in the note names, then fill in the fingerings.

80

DYNAMIC MARKINGS

mf　**mezzo forte**—medium loud

mp　**mezzo piano**—medium soft

MULTIPLE MEASURE REST

$\frac{4}{4}$　　**2**

Count: **1** 2 3 4 ┊ **2** 2 3 4

FADING AWAY

81

EXTENDED RESTS (Duet)

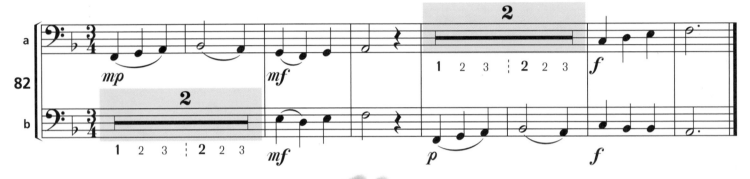

82

a

b

KOOKABURRA (Round)

Australian Folk Song

83

Moderato

① ② ③

FINALE FROM "ORPHEUS" (Can-Can)

Jacques Offenbach
(1819–1880)

84

Vivace

1. 　　2.

ACCENT ON CREATIVITY: *Rhythmic Improvisation*

Improvise your own rhythms in each measure using only the pitches shown.

85

ACCENT ON PERFORMANCE

GALACTIC EPISODE

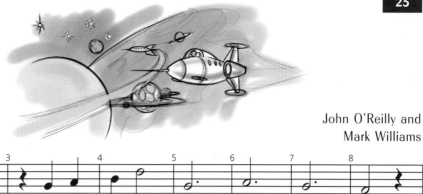

John O'Reilly and
Mark Williams

STACCATO ♩̣ Play the note ½ its normal length.

$$♩̣ \; ♩̣ \; = \; ♪ \text{ 𝄾 } ♪ \text{ 𝄾}$$

TONE BUILDER

86

A SHORT STORY

87

WILLIAM TELL OVERTURE

Gioacchino Rossini
(1792–1868)

Vivace

88

HATIKVAH

Israeli National Anthem

Andante

89

MINUET

Johann Sebastian Bach
(1685–1750)

Moderato

90

1.

2.

ACCENT ON BASSOON

91

For more individual technique practice, see page 43, #6 & 7.

DOTTED QUARTER NOTE

In $\frac{2}{4}$, $\frac{3}{4}$ and $\frac{4}{4}$ time, a dotted quarter note receives 1½ beats.

DOTTED QUARTERS

Count: 1 & 2 & 3 & 4 &

ANVIL CHORUS from "IL TROVATORE" (Duet)

Giuseppe Verdi
(1813–1901)

ALOUETTE

French-Canadian Folk Song

SAKURA

Japanese Folk Song

WEARING OF THE GREEN

Irish Folk Song

ACCENT ON THEORY

TAKE A REST: Complete each measure by adding the correct rest, then write in the counting and clap.

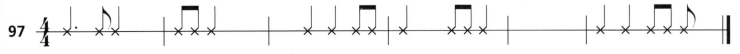

D.S. (DAL SEGNO) AL FINE
Go back to the sign 𝄋 and play until **Fine**.

CLARINET CLIMB

IT'S RAINING, IT'S POURING

Traditional

ARIRANG

Korean Folk Song

ODE TO JOY from "SYMPHONY NO. 9"

Ludwig van Beethoven
(1770–1827)

🅐CCENT ON CREATIVITY: *Free Improvisation*

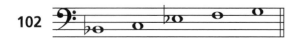

102

Using the five pitches shown, improvise your own melody using any rhythms you know. You may play these notes in any order, repeat notes or use rests.

TEMPO MARKING
Largo
Very slow

D.C. (DA CAPO) AL FINE
Go back to the beginning and
play until **Fine**.

EASY DOES IT

THEME FROM "NEW WORLD SYMPHONY"
Antonin Dvořák
(1841–1904)

SONG OF THE VOLGA BOATMEN
Russian Folk Song

LIZA JANE
American Folk Song

HANSEL AND GRETEL CHORALE
Engelbert Humperdinck
(1854–1921)

ACCENT ON BASSOON

For more individual technique practice, see page 43, #8.

RHYTHM ANTICS

109

mf

Count: 1 & 2 & 1 & 2 &

LONG TIME AGO

American Folk Song

Allegro

110

f

1.

mp

2.

HAIL, THE CONQUERING HERO (Duet)

George F. Handel
(1685–1759)

Moderato

a

111

mf

f

2

b

mf

f

FOLK FESTIVAL

Moderato

112

mp

f

p

f

WE WISH YOU A MERRY CHRISTMAS (Duet)

Traditional Carol

Vivace

a

113

mf

b

mf

ACCENT ON THEORY

114 Arrange the following tempo markings in order from slowest to fastest:

Moderato, Allegro, Andante, Vivace, Largo

_____ _____ _____ _____ _____

slowest - → fastest

ACCENT ON PERFORMANCE

WHEN THE SAINTS GO MARCHING IN

Arr. by John O'Reilly
and Mark Williams

CRESCENDO

get louder gradually

DIMINUENDO

get softer gradually

CROSSING THE BREAK

115

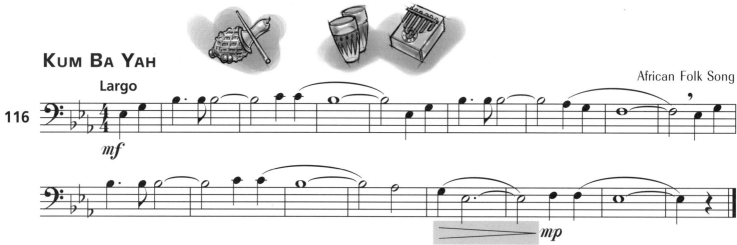

KUM BA YAH

African Folk Song

Largo

116

TRUMPET VOLUNTARY (Duet)

Jeremiah Clarke
(1674–1707)

Moderato

a

117

b

FINLANDIA

Jean Sibelius
(1865–1957)

Andante

118

ACCENT ON CREATIVITY   Create your own composition containing a balance of unity and variety.

119

1. Copy the first two measures into measures 5 and 6 to create unity.
2. Compose new music for the remaining measures to add variety.   3. Play your composition.

TIME SIGNATURE C

Common Time—same as $\frac{4}{4}$

SHEPHERD'S HEY (Duet)

English Folk Song

Allegro

BOTANY BAY

Australian Folk Song

Moderato

REUBEN AND RACHEL (Round)

Traditional

Vivace

AMAZING GRACE

American Folk Song

Andante

ACCENT ON BASSOON

For more individual technique practice, see page 43, #9.

MORE SYNCOPATION

SYNCOPATED RHYTHMS

125

Count: 1 & 2 & 3 & 4 &

RUSSIAN SAILOR'S DANCE

Reinhold Gliere
(1875–1956)

126

YE BANKS AND BRAES OF BONNIE DOON (Duet)

Scottish Folk Song

127

TOM DOOLEY

American Folk Song

128

ACCENT ON THEORY

Arrange the following dynamics in order from softest to loudest and back: *mf*, *p*, *f*, *mp*.

129

KEY SIGNATURE

All B's, E's, A's and D's should be played as Bb, Eb, Ab and Db throughout.

MIXIN' IT UP

ON TOP OF OLD SMOKY

American Folk Song

Allegro

MARCH SLAV

Peter I. Tchaikovsky
(1840–1893)

Largo

LAS MAÑANITAS

Mexican Folk Song

Moderato

POMP AND CIRCUMSTANCE

Edward Elgar
(1857–1934)

Andante

For more individual technique practice, see page 43, #10.

Bassoon Solo

To a Wild Rose
from WOODLAND SKETCHES

Edward MacDowell
(1860–1908)

Andante

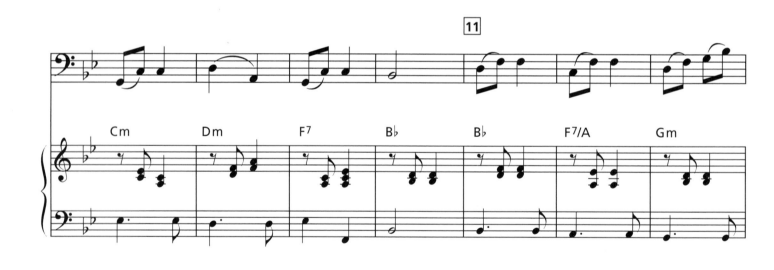

ACCENT ON PERFORMANCE

SOUSA SPECTACULAR

John Philip Sousa
(1854–1932)
Arr. by John O'Reilly
and Mark Williams

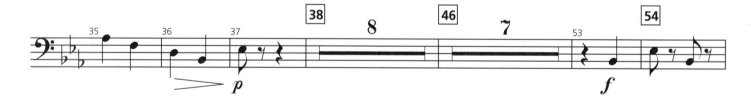

ACCENT ON SCALES

Bb MAJOR SCALE AND CHORDS (Concert Bb)

rit.

F MAJOR SCALE AND CHORDS (Concert F)

rit.

Eb MAJOR SCALE AND CHORDS (Concert Eb)

rit.

Ab MAJOR SCALE AND CHORDS (Concert Ab)

rit.

Bb MAJOR SCALE IN THIRDS (Concert Bb)

Optional articulations:

F MAJOR SCALE IN THIRDS (Concert F)

Eb MAJOR SCALE IN THIRDS (Concert Eb)

Ab MAJOR SCALE IN THIRDS (Concert Ab)

CHROMATIC SCALE

ACCENT ON RHYTHMS

ACCENT ON RESTS

ACCENT ON BASSOON

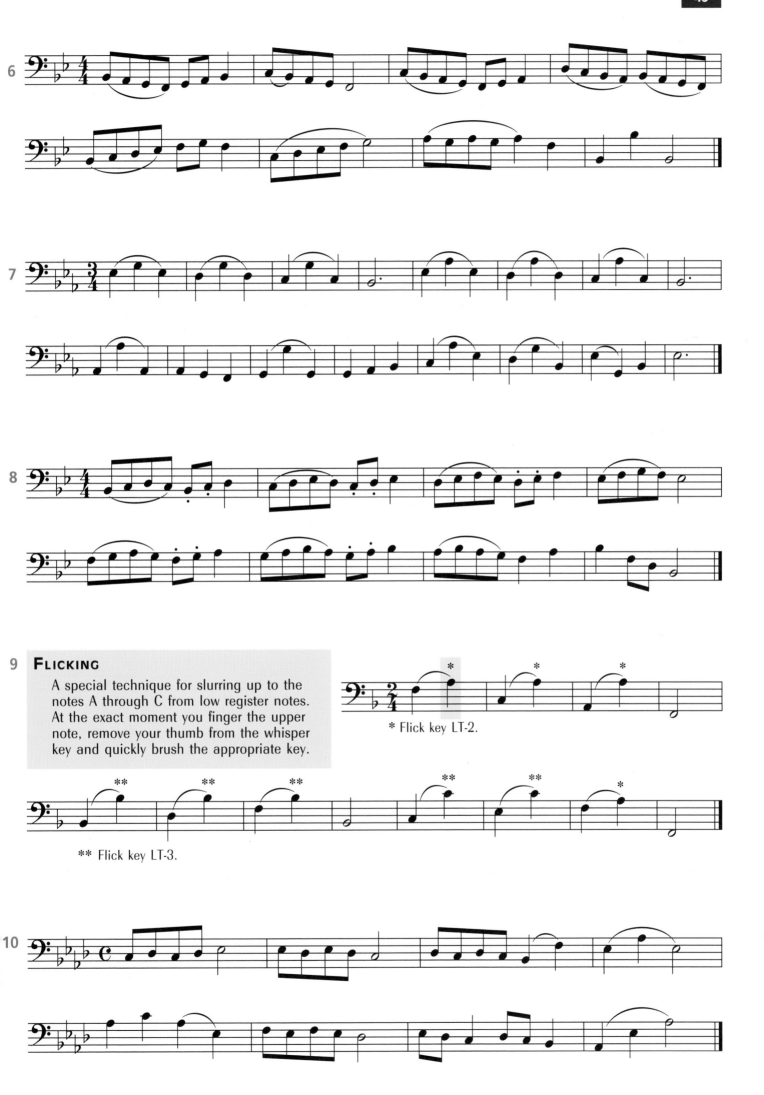

9 **FLICKING**

A special technique for slurring up to the notes A through C from low register notes. At the exact moment you finger the upper note, remove your thumb from the whisper key and quickly brush the appropriate key.

* Flick key LT-2.

** Flick key LT-3.

ACCENT ON CHORALES

CONCERT Bb

Andante

CONCERT F

Largo

CONCERT Eb

Andante

CONCERT Ab

Andante

GLOSSARY

ACCENT (>) Play the note stronger

ALLEGRO Fast tempo

ANDANTE Moderately slow tempo

BACH, JOHANN SEBASTIAN German composer (1685–1750)

BAR LINE Divides the staff into measures

BASS CLEF (𝄢) Also called F clef. The fourth line of the staff is the note F

BEETHOVEN, LUDWIG VAN German composer (1770–1827)

BILLINGS, WILLIAM American composer (1746–1800)

BRAHMS, JOHANNES German composer (1833–1897)

BREATH MARK (') A suggested place to take a breath

CLARKE, JEREMIAH English composer (1674–1707)

COMMON TIME (𝄴) Same as $\frac{4}{4}$ time signature

CRESCENDO (⟨) Get louder gradually

D.C. (DA CAPO) AL FINE Go back to the beginning and play until Fine

DIMINUENDO (⟩) Get softer gradually

DIVISI Some players play the top notes while others play the bottom notes

DOUBLE BAR (‖) The end of a section of music

D.S. (DAL SEGNO) AL FINE Go back to the sign 𝄋 and play until Fine

DUET A composition with parts for two players

DVOŘÁK, ANTONIN Czech composer (1841–1904)

DYNAMIC MARKINGS Symbols that indicate loudness or softness of the music

ELGAR, EDWARD English composer (1857–1934)

FERMATA (⌒) Hold the note longer

1ST AND 2ND ENDINGS Play the 1st ending first time through, then on the repeat, skip to the 2nd ending

FLAT (♭) Lowers the pitch of a note one half step

FORTE (f) Loud

FOSTER, STEPHEN American composer (1826–1864)

GLIERE, REINHOLD Russian composer (1875–1956)

GRIEG, EDVARD Norwegian composer (1843–1907)

HANDEL, GEORGE F. English composer of German birth (1685–1759)

HAYDN, FRANZ JOSEPH Austrian composer (1732–1809)

HUMPERDINCK, ENGELBERT German composer (1854–1921)

INTERNAL REPEAT Repeat only the music between the signs

KEY SIGNATURE Indicates notes which are to be flatted or sharped throughout

LARGO Very slow

LEDGER LINES Used to extend the staff

LILI'UOKALANI Hawaiian composer (1838–1917)

MEASURE The distance between two bar lines

MEZZO FORTE (mf) Medium loud

MEZZO PIANO (mp) Medium soft

MODERATO Medium tempo

MOZART, WOLFGANG A. Austrian composer (1756–1791)

MULTIPLE MEASURE REST Indicates more than one measure of rest

NATURAL (♮) Cancels a flat or sharp until the next bar line

OFFENBACH, JACQUES French composer (1819–1880)

ORCHESTRATION Choosing which instruments play a section of music

PIANO (p) Soft

PICK-UP NOTE(S) Note(s) preceding the first full measure

REPEAT SIGN Play the music again from the beginning

RITARDANDO (RIT.) Gradually slow down the tempo

ROSSINI, GIOACCHINO Italian composer (1792–1868)

ROUND Playing the same music beginning at different times

SHARP (♯) Raises the pitch of a note one half step

SIBELIUS, JEAN Finnish composer (1865–1957)

SLUR Connects notes of different pitch

SOLO One person playing

SOUSA, JOHN PHILIP American composer (1854–1932)

STACCATO (·) Play the note ½ its normal length

STAFF 5 lines and 4 spaces used for writing music

STRAUSS, JOHANN JR. Austrian composer (1825–1899)

SYNCOPATION Starting a note that is one beat or longer on "&"

TCHAIKOVSKY, PETER I. Russian composer (1840–1893)

TEMPO MARKINGS Terms which indicate the speed of the music

TIE Joins two notes of the same pitch to make one long note

TIME SIGNATURE Indicates how many beats are in each measure and what kind of note receives one beat

TREBLE CLEF (𝄞) Also called G clef. The second line of the staff is the note G

VARIATION Changing the rhythm or notes of a theme to create variety

VERDI, GIUSEPPE Italian composer (1813–1901)

VIVACE Very fast tempo

Bassoon fingering chart

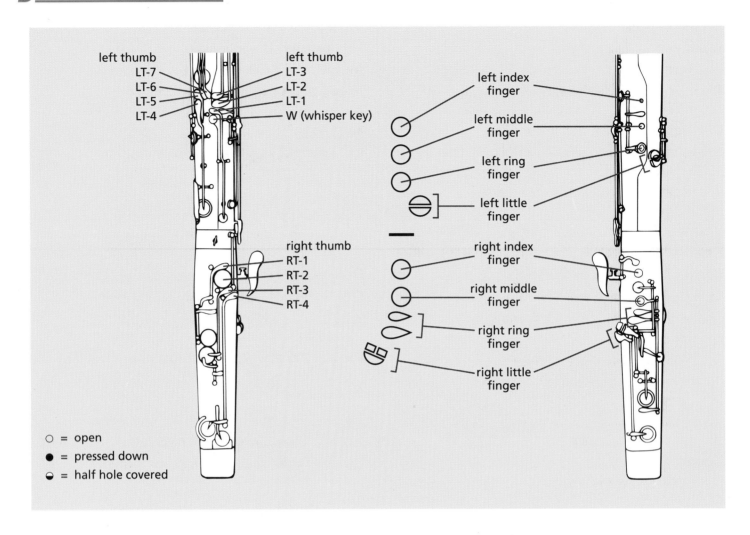

○ = open

● = pressed down

◒ = half hole covered

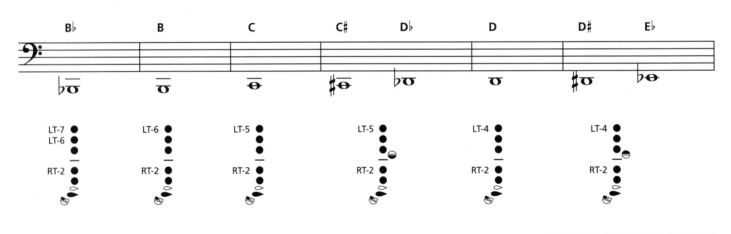

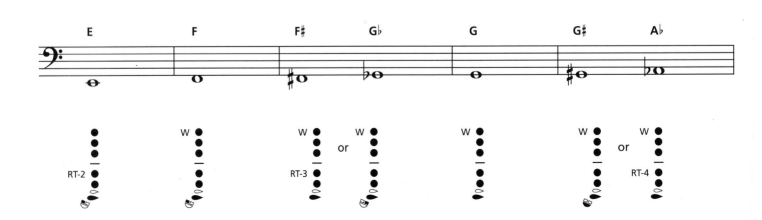

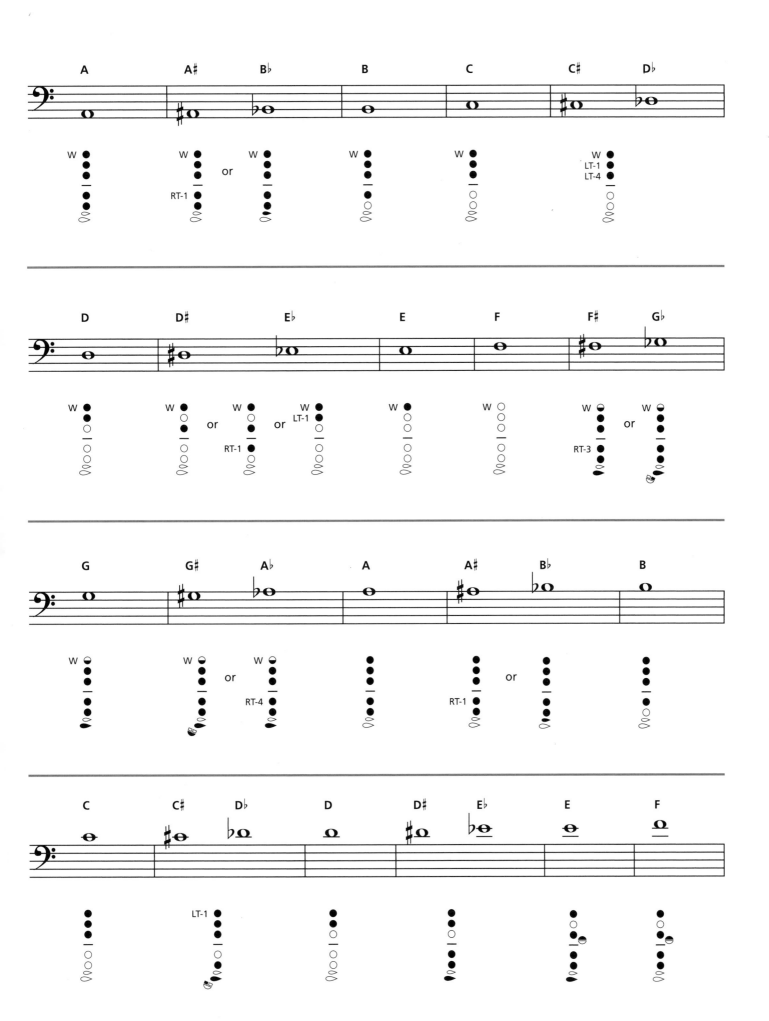

HOME PRACTICE RECORD

Week	Date	ASSIGNMENT	Mon	Tue	Wed	Thur	Fri	Sat	Sun	Total	Parent Signature
1											
2											
3											
4											
5											
6											
7											
8											
9											
10											
11											
12											
13											
14											
15											
16											
17											
18											
19											
20											
21											
22											
23											
24											
25											
26											
27											
28											
29											
30											
31											
32											
33											
34											
35											
36	Date	ASSIGNMENT	Mon	Tue	Wed	Thur	Fri	Sat	Sun	Total	Parent Signature